Marx's *Capital*

BEN FINE

Lecturer in Economics, Birkbeck College,
University of London

First edition 1975
Reprinted 1977 , 1979

Published by
THE MACMILLAN PRESS LTD
London and Basingstoke
Associated companies in Delhi Dublin
Hong Kong Johannesburg Lagos Melbourne
New York Singapore and Tokyo

ISBN 0 333 17845 9

Printed in Hong Kong

Contents

Acknowledgements

This book is prepared from courses given at Birkbeck College on 'Marxist Economics' and 'The Distribution of Income and Wealth'. I have been influenced by those who taught and attended those courses. Bob Rae and Simon Mohun read earlier versions and have made many suggestions that I have incorporated. I thank those who have given help, but retain sole responsibility for the contents.

MARX TO ENGELS

'The best points in my book are: (1) the *double character of labour*, according to whether it is expressed in use value or exchange value...(2) the treatment of *surplus value independently of its particular* forms as profit, interest, ground rent, etc.'

Selected Correspondence, Letter 99 (Lawrence & Wishart, London, 1934).

MARX TO J. WEYDEMEYER

'And now to myself, no credit is due to me for discovering the existence of classes in modern society or the struggle between them. Long before the bourgeois historians had described the historical development of this class struggle and bourgeois economists the economic anatomy of the classes. What I did that was new was to prove: (1) that the *existence of classes* is only bound up with *particular historical phases in the development of production*, (2) that the class struggle necessarily leads to *the dictatorship of the proletariat*, (3) that this dictatorship itself only constitutes the transition to the *abolition of all classes* and to a *classless society*.'

Marx and Engels, *Selected Works* (Lawrence & Wishart, London, 1968) p. 679.

1 Introduction

This book is both an introduction to and an interpretation of Marx's three volumes of *Capital*. On neither count could it be a substitute for reading *Capital*, but hopefully it will stimulate and help some to study it. Nevertheless, although faced by the constraints of space, I have undertaken an ambitious task and this has some important consequences.

The text here is very condensed in order to obtain maximum coverage. This means that it may be necessary to read some sections more than once and give careful thought to the arguments presented. Naturally I have attempted to include the most significant aspects of *Capital*, but inevitably many important problems have been omitted. Throughout the book I have refrained from quoting Marx directly. This has imposed the discipline of putting his argument in my own words. However, Marx's style is so powerful, that I apologise in advance if my own wording has closely echoed his own in places.

After a brief discussion of Marx's method I have followed Volume i of *Capital* fairly closely. I include a chapter on the genesis of capitalism, with which Marx concluded Volume i. This interrupts the flow of argument from the general analysis of capital to crisis and distribution theory. Unfortunately this cannot be avoided, since theory, unlike history, cannot always unfold chronologically.

The remainder of the book, whilst covering Volumes ii and iii, contains more of my own invention. The industrial circuit of capital is explicitly used to describe crises, and the largest chapter is devoted to unravelling Marx's lengthy treatment of distribution. The final chapter, which sketches an interpretation of modern capitalism, is by far the most difficult. For it I have drawn extensively on the debates within the Conference of Socialist Economists, but would probably find all the participants in disagreement with me on one aspect or another.

This book was written for undergraduates in economies. They should gain most benefit, since I have used Marx's analysis to expose the limited nature of orthodox economies. However, non-economists should also be able to follow the text without difficulty.

2 Method

Marx's methodology can usefully be described as one of abstraction and successive approximation. By 'abstraction' we mean extracting the essentials, not being purely theoretical or divorced from reality. The process of successive approximation does not really mean moving closer to a better 'solution', but the building of explanations of phenomena on the structure of the essentials. If these explanations are impossible in terms of modification or extension of the first stage of abstract analysis, this implies the essentials themselves are inadequate and need to be changed.

As a methodology this is hardly controversial and does not need much elaboration. What is important is the content given to the methodology that is Marx's method, and the intended scope of its application. In his pursuit of the revolutionary transformation of society it was Marx's purpose to uncover the general process of historical change, to apply this understanding to particular types of societies, and finally to make concrete studies of particular historical situations. To understand how he did this it is convenient to study what Lenin described as the three component parts of Marxism, which were the culmination of early nineteenth-century intellectual development – German philosophy, French socialism and British political economy. In this section we discover how Marx's philosophy and socialism led to his understanding of the general process of historical change. His application of this and his exploitation of British political economy in the study

13

of capitalist society is the subject of the remainder of the book.

Marx was born in Germany in 1818 and began an early university career studying law. His interest quickly turned to philosophy, which at that time was dominated by Hegel and his disciples. They were idealists and believed that the study of man's consciousness was the key to the understanding of society. (This was their abstraction. Just as science leads to the development of technology, so intellectual progress is the basis for the advance of government, culture and the other forms of social life.) Historically man progressed towards the Idea, the perfection of institutions, culture, religion, and hence society. History was a dramatic stage on which institutions and ideas battled for hegemony. For Hegel this conflict was ever present, the existing state of affairs always contained a tension with what it was becoming. Each stage of development contained the seeds of transformation to a higher stage. Each stage was an advance on those that had preceded it, but it absorbed elements from them. This process of change, in which new ideas did not so much defeat the old as resolve conflicts within them, Hegel called the *dialectic*.

Hegel died in 1831. When Marx was still a young man at university, two opposed groups of Hegelians, Young and Old (radical and reactionary), both claimed to be Hegel's legitimate successors. The Old Hegelians believed that Prussian absolute monarchy, religion, and society represented the triumphant achievement of the Idea in its dialectical progress. In contrast the Young Hegelians, dangerously anti-religious, believed that intellectual development had far to advance. This set the stage for a battle between the two schools, each side believing a victory heralded the progress of German society. Marx, having observed the absurdity, poverty and degradation of much of German life, identified himself initially with the Young Hegelians. For the participants the great debate, conducted as philosophy, transcended politics. The struggles of the real world paled to insignificance against the advance to be made in ideas.

Marx's sympathy for the Young Hegelians was extremely short-lived, largely because of the influence on him of Feuerbach, who was a materialist. By this we do not mean he was crudely interested in his own welfare, being in fact sacked from a university position for his views. He believed that far from man's consciousness dominating his life and existence, it was man himself who determined his consciousness. In *The Essence of Christianity* Feuerbach mounted a simple but brilliant polemic against religion. Man needed God because religion satisfied an emotional need. To satisfy this need, man had projected his best qualities on to a God figure, worshipping what had been made to the extent that God had assumed an independent existence in human consciousness. To regain his humanity man needed to substitute the love of his fellow men for the love of God.

Marx was immediately struck by this insight. Initially he criticised Feuerbach for seeing man as an individual struggling to fulfil his human nature, rather than as a social being. However he soon moved beyond Feuerbach's rather crude materialism. He did this in two different ways. First, he extended Feuerbach's materialist philosophy to all dominant ideas prevailing in society, that is to say to ideology and man's conception of the society in which he lived. Secondly, he extended Feuerbach's ideas to history. Feuerbach's analysis had been entirely ahistorical and non-dialectical. Man satisfied a 'material' emotional need through religion. But the origin of that need remained unexplained, even if we could explain the idea by the need. Marx saw the solution to this problem in man's material condition, in other words the way in which production was organised. This was the abstraction that he made. In contrast to the Hegelian dialectical progress of ideas, Marx took the contradiction between the forces of production and the relations of production (described below) as the motive force of historical change. Man's consciousness was critical in Marx's thought, but it could only be understood in relation to man's historical, social and material situation.

In 1845–6 when he was writing *The German Ideology* with Engels and the *Theses on Feuerbach*, Marx had already begun to be influenced by the ideas of the French socialists. These ideas, fostered by the heritage of the French Revolution and the failure of emerging bourgeois society to realise the demands of *'liberté, egalité et fraternité'*, were dominated by class politics and often included belief in the necessity and possibility of revolutionary seizure of power. Socialism has many different meanings to different people and political movements. For Marx, socialism was more than an idealised reorganisation of society and was certainly not a programme for reforms for capitalism. He believed that a socialist society, in which classes would eventually disappear, would be based on the productive power developed by capitalism, organised according to a plan formed by the full decision-making participation of working people.

However, central to Marx's socialism is the notion that it is the proletariat which is going to make the ultimate change in the order of material life. Socialism is the identification with this class and with its struggles. Marx had little time for utopian socialists or others (except to condemn them vehemently) who envisaged or idealised a new structure for society without seeing the means for its attainment: revolution by the proletariat. This perspective gave him the key to all history, most simply stated in *The Communist Manifesto*, as 'The history of all hitherto existing society is the history of class struggles.' How easy to identify the proletariat's task of overthrowing capitalist society once history was seen as the outcome of class struggle! Conversely the class antagonisms that Marx perceived in society in his own time cannot have failed to suggest to him the application of class analysis to previous epochs.

Marx's method for studying the general process of historical change was essentially complete. He called it the materialist conception of history and never used the terms 'historical' or 'dialectical' materialism, which were coined by Engels. He gives an excellent description of this method in the *Preface to a Contribution to a Critique of Political Economy*. We now tie these remarks together.

In organising production men enter into relations with each other – as capitalist or wage-earner, as slave or master, or as lord or serf. These relations exist independently of their choice even though they have been historically made by man in his own development. The relations of production specific to a particular mode of production, for example capitalism or feudalism, are best studied as class relations in all but the most simple societies. They are the basis on which the whole of society is constructed with limited variability. Definite forms of political, legal and intellectual life correspond to definite modes of production. Just as freedom to buy and sell are key legal characteristics of capitalist society, so divine or feudal obligation are the legal foundations of feudalism.

One individual's reflection on his situation and society will have little influence on the pattern of choices open to him. His pattern of life is most severely constrained and defined for him by existing social conditions, in particular the places to be filled in the process of production. In addition a self-justifying superstructure of political, legal, intellectual and distributional forms have also already been established, and these in general blinker and discourage all but the most conventional views of society, whether by physical force or force of habit. In entering the relations of production man inevitably finds in his social existence, his practical day-to-day life, the unconscious rationale for the system. The serf feels bound by loyalty to master and king. The wage-earner has freedom to sell his labour. He can strive for higher wages, but does not question the wage system.

This all demonstrates the stability existing in a given mode of production. The crucial questions are how can that stability be threatened and how can the will to change the system of production be generated. Society can be seen in a new light, and not as immortal, only when the conditions of production are disrupted. When the duke is unable to fulfil his feudal obligation or the worker unable to sell his labour, then feudalism or capitalism may be challenged. This occurs historically when the forces of production, crudely the technological ability to produce, are held back by the relations of production. The forces of production tend to be dynamic, changing frequently and placing great strains on the relations of production which are sluggish and inflexible. Manufacturing is impossible under feudal relations as is efficiency and profit maximising. Attempts to accommodate the forces of production within the existing relations brings a breakdown in those relations, and with this down falls the old superstructure of ideology, and so on. These changes do not come about overnight but are contained in a century of progress, and stumbling. The development of the relation of production depends upon the outcome of class struggle. The ruling class of any mode of production always resists the advance of the conditions favourable to the class that is to be dominant in the new society. Working people will be torn between two competing systems of oppression, until under capitalism they constitute the emerging ruling class.

MARX'S ECONOMICS

Given his conception of history, it was natural for Marx to turn his study to economics in analysing capitalism. To do this he immersed himself in British political economy, in particular developing the labour theory of value from the value theory of Smith and Ricardo. For Marx, however, it was insufficient to base the source of value in exchange on labour-time of production as had Ricardo. This takes for granted the existence of exchange, prices and commodities. That commodities are more valuable because they embody more labour, begs the question of why there are commodities at all, let alone whether it is a relevant abstraction to assume they exchange at their labour cost of production. This anticipates the following chapter, but it illustrates a key feature of his method and a common criticism by Marx of other writers. Marx found other economists not so much wrong as inadequate. He was interested in probing beneath the appearance of society to the reality below. This meant taking nothing for granted; leaving no important phenomena of society unexplained. What economists tend to assume as timeless features of men and societies, Marx was determined to root out and understand.

Marx did take for granted, as part of human nature, the need to produce and consume. The way in which production was organised had to be revealed, and the dependence of other social relations on this explained first structurally and then historically. For example Marx castigated the utilitarians for their assumption that certain characteristics of human behaviour, like greed, were permanent features of 'human nature', when they were characteristics generated in individuals by

18

particular societies. To distinguish man's possible relations with the physical world from those induced with it and other men, Marx spoke of Nature and nature respectively. It was part of Marx's task as well as his method to explain man's nature, and throughout this book we shall attempt to understand how men view economic relations and behave accordingly.

Clearly Marx's economics, in contrast to much contemporary orthodox economics, is a social science in that it concerns itself with the relations that men set between themselves, rather than with the technical relationships between things and with the art of economising. Marx was not interested then in constructing a price theory, a set of efficiency criteria, or a series of welfare propositions. These would depend upon assuming a limited potential for society to change and standards of welfare rooted within the framework of that society.

This is not to suggest that Marxism contains no normative content. Rather, like any theory interpretative of society and thus of men and their social relations, it is an amalgam of positive and normative judgements, to disentangle which would be an endless task. Indeed the separation of positive and normative theory so popular in modern economics is an impossible one for Marx beyond the trivial, whether purely empirical or wildly utopian. On the one hand statistical relationships, even if value free, can provide no theory of causation without interpretation of the society from which they are drawn. On the other hand the application and meaningfulness of normative propositions depends upon their possible fulfilment. Investigating this requires the unravelling of the social, political and economic ties that bind societies. Economists who maintain a distinction between positive and normative inevitably take for granted those features of capitalist society that Marx felt it necessary to explain: the private ownership of the means of production, their operation for and distribution by exchange, with remuneration involving the economic categories of prices, profits and wages.

3 Commodity Production

THE LABOUR THEORY OF VALUE

In analysing a mode of production, for example capitalism, Marx's starting point was always production. In any society the object of production is use-values, that is to say useful things. Thus the production of use-values can be taken for granted, just as production itself can be. In addition, at the first level of abstraction, Marx felt it unnecessary to explain the distribution of use-values in production, that is, the relative quantities of each product produced. This would depend upon a whole host of influences, for example ideology, technology, and the distribution of income, which could only be studied themselves after the basic relations of production had been uncovered. Contrast this with modern economics with its neutral government and given utility functions and factor endowments.

One fundamental feature of capitalism is that it is a highly developed system of commodity production. Following Adam Smith, Marx distinguished use-value from exchange-value: usefulness, which cannot be quantified, from the ability to exchange with other commodities, which can be quantified. Every commodity has a use-value, but not every use-value is a commodity, for use-values, which are either freely available or are not exchanged, have no exchange-value (for example air and production for personal use).

Marx saw exchange-value as embodying a numerical equivalence relationship between objects, at first in the abstract. This relationship had to satisfy certain properties, which become familiar to us at school and in daily life. If x exchanges for y ($x \sim y$ say), then $2x \sim 2y$. If, in addition, $u \sim v$, then (u and x) $\sim$ (v and y), and so on.

But there are an unlimited number of relationships between objects satisfying these properties, for example weight, volume. The question Marx wanted to answer is what is the determinant of the relationship of exchange of commodities. What is the thing common to two commodities that causes them to be equivalents in exchange? In the case of weight or volume, equivalence is due to a physical or natural property, namely mass and size respectively. However, although every commodity is characterised by its particular physical properties which give it its use-value, its exchange-value has no systematic relation to these properties. Even the most useful things, air, sun and water, often have little or no exchange-value. What creates the relationship of exchange is not a physical relationship but an historically specific social one, the relationship between commodities as the product of men's labour. This will be clarified below.

For Marx it was an incontrovertible fact that throughout history men had lived by their labour. Further, beyond the most simple societies, some men had always lived without working, by the labour of other men. However, this appropriation of one man's labour by another took different forms and was justified in different ways in different societies. Under feudalism the mode of distribution of produce was often by direct appropriation justified by feudal or even divine right. Under capitalism produce was distributed by the free exchange of commodities, and so the free exchange of the products of men's labour. How this freedom could bring about an appropriation of the labour of one class by another will be discussed in the next chapter. For the moment we are only interested in the nature of the exchange relationship.

We have seen that a commodity necessarily contains a use-value, but a use-value is not a commodity unless it embodies a labour cost (and is exchanged). Thus, the property that all commodities have in common, that creates the relationship of exchange, is that they are the product of labour. This is the basis of the labour theory of value, and it embodies a social relationship which can easily be theoretically quantified by

21

analysing exchange from the viewpoint of the labour-time necessary to produce commodities. The labour theory of value is not a metaphysical notion, despite the impossibility of empirically calculating values, for it expresses definite facts about material life. For the same reason, nor is it a purely ethical theory, despite its view of man as producer rather than abstainer, sinner or factor of production.

Marx realised that under capitalism, where exchange of commodities is pervasive, production is for exchange and not for immediate use. Capitalism is a system in which the aim of production is social use-values – use-values for others unknown because of the anonymity of the market. The production of social use-values and exchange is intimately linked. But just as products embody social use-values, so they are created by social labour in the abstract. Thus, what exchange represents is the exchange of the products of individual concrete labour treated as abstract social labour. Exchange is not interested in quality (type) of labour but only in quantity, and that quantity is of abstract social labour.

This is not to suggest that commodities do exchange at their values, the labour-time necessary to produce them taking account both of direct (living) labour inputs and indirect (dead) labour inputs (the labour-time necessary to produce produced means of production, i.e. raw materials and fixed machinery). Market prices will be modified by differing capital–labour ratios, scarcities, skills, monopolies, and tastes. These influences have been the prime object of study of orthodox economists since the neoclassical revolution of the 1870s, with little advance being made on Adam Smith's ideas of the 1770s. They were not ignored by Marx, but they are irrelevant, as we shall see, for uncovering the social relations of production specific to capitalism. If this cannot be done on the assumption that commodities exchange at their values, it certainly cannot be done in the more complicated case when they do not. Throughout, unless otherwise stated, we shall assume that commodities exchange at their values. This is not to be interpreted as a fully fledged price theory.

Thus, capitalism, as general commodity production, is characterised by the production of social use-values and hence the exchange of the products of individual concrete labour expressed, in exchange, as abstract social labour. Marx's labour theory of value incorporates a social relation: the exchange of the products of individual concrete labour. As a price theory it is at best a poor approximation, but the important point is that the relationship between exchange, prices and values is not purely quantitative, it reflects definite social relations of production and distribution. It is these that must be understood. It is worth noting that a labour theory of value only occurred and could only occur historically, when commodity production, that is to say exchange of labour-products, had developed sufficiently. Certainly changing ideas reflected changing relations of distribution, but it is the capitalist relations of production in which we are interested. We can now turn to these having understood the nature of commodity exchange.

LABOUR AND LABOUR-POWER

In the exchange of commodities we have seen that the exchange of different types of labour products takes place. This could occur without capitalism, if independent artisans exchanged their products. Marx called such a situation simple commodity production. It is more a logical possibility than ever an historically realised dominant mode of production. What characterises capitalism is not just the exchange of the different products of the different labourers, but the purchase and sale of the labourer's ability to work. To distinguish the labourer's work from his ability or capacity to work, Marx called the former his labour but the latter his labour-power. Under capitalism labour-power becomes a commodity, the purchaser is the capitalist, the seller is the labourer. The price of labour-power is the wage. The labourer sells his labour-power to the capitalist, who determines how that labour-power should be exercised as labour to produce particular commodities. As a commodity, labour-power must have a use-value, and this is that it is the creator of use-values. This is a property independent of the particular society in which production takes place. However, under capitalism, use-values are produced in the form of

23

commodities and, as such, embody abstract labour-time or value. Thus, labour-power as a commodity also has the use-value of creating value. In this it is unique (note that use-values, but not values, can also be created naturally). Labour-power, the creator of specific use-values in commodity form and hence the creator of value, is the commodity that must be bought by the capitalist. Then he, not the labourer or producer, owns and sells the produced use-values as commodities.

The labourer is not therefore a slave in the conventional sense of the word. He is not sold like other commodities, but he sells his labour-power himself. Also the length of time for which the sale is made is often very short. Yet in many other respects the labourer is like a slave. He has no control, or little, over his labour process or product. He is free to refuse to sell his labour-power, but this is a limited freedom, the alternative in the limit being starvation or social degradation. One could as well argue that a slave could refuse to work. For this reason the labourer under capitalism is best described as a wage-slave.

On the other side is the capitalist. He controls the labourer and his product by his command of wage payments and his ownership of the labourers' tools and raw materials or means of production. This is the key to the property relations specific to capitalism. For it is the capitalist class's monopoly of the means of production, which ties the labourer to wage-slavery. If the labourer owned or was entitled to use the means of production, he would hardly sell his labour-power rather than his product on the market, given the profit made by the capitalist. Now we see that the labour theory of value not only captures the distributional relationship of the exchange of labour products, but also embodies the more fundamental relations of production specific to capitalism, once the distinction between labour and labour-power is drawn. The social exchange of labour-power, in addition to the exchange of the products of labour, presupposes the monopoly of the means of production on the one hand and the existence of a class of wage-labourers on the other. Naturally it is precisely this distinction which is never drawn in orthodox economics with its 'neutral' terminology of factor inputs and outputs.

THE FETISHISM OF COMMODITIES

Marx was able to see that in the exchange of produced use-values the exchange of labour products took place, but to many of his contemporary economists and to nearly all subsequent ones, this relationship between men and their labour remains merely a relationship between things, that is to say 1 coat = 2 pairs of shoes. Thus, whilst capitalism organises production in definite social relationships between men, these relationships are expressed and appear as relationships between things. Marx called such a perspective on the capitalist world the fetishism of commodities. It is most apparent in modern economics, where even labour-power is treated as an input or factor like any other. Factor rewards are seen first and foremost as due to the physical properties of the factors, as if land or machinery could produce rent or profit rather than men existing together in particular relationships in particular societies.

Marx drew the brilliant parallel between commodity fetishism and feudal religious devotion. God is man's own creation. Under feudalism, man's relationship with God concealed and justified his actual relationship to his fellow men, an absurd bond of exploitation and slavery as it appears to the *bourgeois* mind. Capitalism, however, has its own God and bible. The relationship of exchange between things is also created by man, concealing the true relationship of exploitation and justifying this by the religious doctrine of freedom of exchange.

Commodity fetishism characterises people's outlook in general, worker and capitalist alike, and this can be made the basis of a theory of alienation. Not only is the worker divorced from the control of his product and the process of producing it, but his view of this situation is distorted. The capitalist is subject to the control of exchange and profit-making. For both, it appears that things exert this control, and not the social relations of production peculiar to capitalism. For example, the loss of employment or bankruptcy with subsequent poverty may be blamed on a thing or impersonal force, for example the unfortunate breakdown of a machine.

25

Marx's concept of commodity fetishism forges a link with his earlier work of 1844. Then, whilst breaking with Hegelian idealism and adopting a materialist philosophy, he developed a theory of alienation. This concentrated on the individual and his relation to his physical and mental activity, his fellow men and his consciousness of these processes.

In *Capital*, after extensive economic study, Marx is able to make explicit the social coercive forces exerted by capitalist society on the individual. These can be the compulsion of profitability and wage slavery or the more subtle distortions by which these forces are ideologically justified: abstinence, the work ethic, freedom of exchange, and commodity fetishism. Unlike other theories of alienation, a Marxist theory places the individual in his class position and analyses his perception of that position. He is not seen, in the first instance, as a powerless individual in an unexplained 'system' of irrationality, impersonality, inequality, authoritarianism, bureaucracy or whatever. These phenomena have their own character and function in capitalist society at a particular time. They can only be understood as a whole or in relation to individuals against the perspective of the needs of capital at that time. It is to these needs that we now turn.

4 Capital and Exploitation

EXCHANGE

We have emphasised that the production of use-values in commodity form tends to conceal the social relationships of production between men and their labour by concentrating attention on exchange relationships between things. Nevertheless, as simple commodity production demonstrates logically and a history of trade demonstrates in reality, exchange itself can exist without capitalism. It is when labour-power itself becomes a commodity that the seeds of capitalism are sown. In this chapter, by examining exchange from the perspectives of a worker (or more generally a consumer) and then a capitalist, we will see why this must be so.

Essential to exchange, beyond simple bartering, is money. The functions of money have been well explored. It is a unit of account, a means of payment, and a store of value. We rely upon the first function throughout this book. As a means of payment it mediates the process of exchange. (Note that, at any one time, this use conflicts with its use as a store of value, and this is important in crises. For the moment we are interested in exchange only.)

Consider an individual who owns some commodity but would prefer to exchange it for another. First the commodity must be exchanged for money. We represent this by $C–M$. Secondly the money obtained is exchanged for the desired commodity, $M–C$. Commodities are advanced for money in order to purchase different commodities, and this can be represented by $C–M–C$, the circulation of commodities. We denote the two extremes of the circulation by C because they

27

are in commodity form and they have the same value, not because they are the same thing. Indeed they cannot be the same thing, otherwise the whole purpose of the exchange is defeated. Given no cheating, there is no gain or loss of value in any of the transactions, each of which, in principle, could be reversed. This is summarised in Fig. 1.

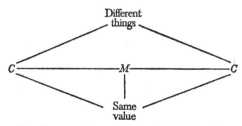

FIG. 1. Simple commodity exchange – selling in order to buy

Typically, under capitalism, this simple commodity exchange could start with a labourer. The only commodity he has to sell is his labour-power, and this is his means of consumption, by its exchange for wages (M) and eventually wage-goods (C). Alternatively the exchange could be undertaken by a capitalist. He realises the value of produced commodities on the market, and can then purchase raw materials and labour-power to renew production or buy consumption goods.

CAPITAL

A capitalist starts with money. With this he purchases commodities of a special type, means of production, or inputs, including labour-power (M-C). A necessary condition for this is the willingness on the part of the labourer to sell his labour-power. This willingness, an exercise of the 'freedom' of exchange, is forced on the labourer. Selling labour-power becomes, on the one hand, a condition of work. It is the only access to the means of production monopolised by capitalists. On the other hand it is a condition of consumption, as it is the only commodity that labour is able to sell.

Having gathered together his inputs the capitalist organises production and sells the resulting output. In this he eventually retrieves the money from *C–M*. The dash here conceals the intervention of production in the transformation of the inputs into money, and this will be discussed in Chapter 7. For the moment, we can represent a capitalist's exchange activity by *M–C–M*. In contrast to simple commodity exchange the circulation begins and ends with money, not commodities. This implies that at the two extremes is the same thing, not different things. The only purpose then in undertaking this exchange activity is to get more, not different. If less were the objective, money could be thrown away without any palaver. The motive of exchange is to expand value, and so we replace the final *M* by *M'*. *M'* is numerically greater than *M*, $M' - M = m$, for example.

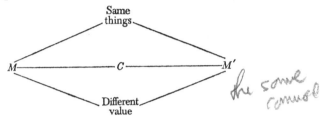

FIG. 2. Capitalist exchange – buying in order to sell dearer (contrast with FIG. 1)

Money only acts as capital when it is used to generate more money. The purpose and nature of capital is to act as self-expanding value. An understanding of this allows capital to be distinguished from the various forms it assumes and the functions undertaken by those forms, whether it be as money, commodity or factor input. Each of these is capital only in so far as it contributes directly toward the self-expansion of value. As such it can function as capital, as well as performing its function as means of payment, depository of exchange-value, or means of production.

We have characterised capital as self-expanding value by examining the exchange activity of an industrial capitalist. There are other forms of capital though, namely merchant capital and loan capital. Both of these also expand value by buying (merchandise or bonds rather than means of production) in order to sell dearer. Both appear historically before industrial capital. It was Marx's insight to reverse historical

29

appearance and analyse capitalism in its pure form, without the complication of mercantilism or usury. By assuming that no value is created in exchange, Marx was able to show that capitalism can rely upon the exchange of equal values. Its secrets must lie in production and not in exchange. We follow his example and accommodate other forms of capital in Chapter 9. This abstraction is borne out historically by the relative increase of industrial capital, but it in no way relegates finance or commerce to the insignificant.

EXPLOITATION

Most economists might find this characterisation of capital as self-expanding value uncontroversial, even if a little odd and unnecessary. In Fig. 2 we see that although M and M' have different values, M and C have the same value. This implies that in the movement $C-M'$, extra value has been created. Marx called this added value 'surplus value'; numerically it equals m and this is the difference between the values of inputs and outputs. It is not the existence of surplus value (profit in its money form) that is controversial, but the explanation of its source. We have already located the source of surplus in production by assuming that exchange does not create any value. This means that among the commodities (C) purchased by the capitalist there must be one or more that creates in production more value than it costs. However, we have already established the labour theory of value as the appropriate analytical tool to reflect the social exchange of commodities that characterises capitalist production. The search for the commodities that produce surplus value is now limited to those that contribute more labour-time (value) to outputs during production than they cost to produce as inputs. This leaves just one candidate – labour-power.

First, let us consider the other inputs. Whilst they contribute value to output as a result of the labour-time that has been necessary to produce them in the past, the quantity of value (labour-time) that they add to output is no more nor less than that past labour-time, that is to say their own value or cost.

Non-labour inputs cannot transfer more value to outputs than they cost as inputs. Now consider labour-power. Its value is the cost of its purchase, which, in real terms, is no more nor less than the labour-time necessary to produce the real wage, a subsistence bundle of commodities. The value it creates in production is the quantity of labour-time exercised in return for that wage. Unlike the other inputs, there is no reason why the contribution made by labour-power to the value of output should equal the cost of labour-power. Indeed it can only be because the value of labour-power is less than labour-time contributed that surplus value is created. From a purely logical point of view the wage could exceed labour-time contributed, giving 'negative surplus value'. If this happened one would find that there would be an abrupt halt in the use of money as capital, as it could no longer function as self-expanding value.

We have demonstrated by using labour-time as our unit of account that, for capital to fulfil its role as self-expanding value, the value contributed by a labourer to output exceeds the remuneration he receives for his labour-power. The labour theory of value is forced upon us because we are analysing commodity exchange. Capitalism, under which not only the products of labour but also labour-power becomes a commodity, must produce surplus value, and this must be created by the excess of labour-time over the value of labour-power. Labour-power not only creates use-values and value, it also creates surplus value. The strength of this argument is seen by its brief comparison with alternative theories of value.

Theories of abstinence, waiting, or intertemporal preference depend upon the sacrifice by capitalists of present consumption as the source of profits. Nobody could deny that these 'sacrifices' (usually made in luxurious comfort) are a condition of profit, but like thousands of other conditions they are not a cause of profits. People without capital could abstain, wait, and make intertemporal choices until they were blue in the face without creating profits for themselves. It is not abstinence that creates capital, but capital that requires abstinence. Waiting has existed in all societies, it is even to be found among squirrels. Similar remarks apply to viewing risk as a source of profit. It must always be borne in mind that it is not things, abstract or otherwise, that create economic categories, for example profits or wages, but definite social relations between men.

Marginal productivity theories explain the increase in value between C and M' by the contributions to output by every input. Such a theory can contain no social content, except to reflect *bourgeois* values. Labour is treated on a par with other *things*. Factors of production have existed in all societies, but the same cannot be said of profits, wages, rents or even prices. No distinction can be drawn between simple commodity exchange and capitalism, because labour-power and labour are not distinguished, there being no interest in the social organisation of production but only in quantities of means of production.

All value is created by labour then, but all surplus value is created by the exploitation of immediate, direct or living labour. Suppose a labourer works a ten-hour day, but that the necessary labour-time to produce his wage is five hours. Then for five hours each day he works 'free' for the capitalist. In this case the rate of exploitation defined as the ratio of surplus to necessary labour-time is 5/5 equals 1 or 100 per cent. Note that this definition could be applied to modes of production other than capitalism, for example feudalism with feudal dues or slavery. In these last two cases the fact of exploitation is apparent, it is only under capitalism that exploitation in production is veiled by the freedom of exchange. Marx referred to the rate of surplus value when being specific about exploitation under capitalism.

Denote surplus labour-time by s, and necessary labour time by v, called variable capital. The rate of exploitation, $e = s/v$. v is called variable capital because its value varies during production, contributing more value to output than it costs as an input. It is variable in contrast to constant capital (c). This is not capital fixed in production (a factory) but raw materials and wear and tear on fixed capital. It is constant capital, because its value does not vary during production but is preserved in output by the labourer, a service he unwittingly performs for the capitalist. c and v are both capital because they represent value, in money form, advanced by capitalists. The value λ of any one commodity is made up of constant and variable capital and surplus value, $\lambda = c + v + s$. Its cost is $c + v$, leaving the surplus value (s) to form profit in money form.

The total amount of surplus value produced for a capitalist depends directly on the rate of exploitation and the total amount of labour he employs. The latter can be increased by accumulation (see Chapter 5). Assume that real wages remain unchanged. The rate of exploitation can be increased in two ways, and attempts to increase it will be made – for the nature of capital as self-expanding value imposes an important qualitative objective on its agents: profit maximisation. Firstly e can be increased on the basis of existing technology to produce absolute surplus value by increasing the length of the working day. There are severe limits to this process, given twenty-four hours in a day. Nevertheless it is always important in the early phases of capitalist development, and at any time it is a remedy for low profitability – if the medicine can be administered.

The development of capitalism brings the production of relative surplus value as the dominant method of increasing e. This occurs through technological change, whereby the value of labour-power (v) is reduced by cheapening the labour cost of the wage. There are many mechanisms for doing this, co-operation and finer division of labour, use of machinery and factories, increasing the pace of work, and scientific discovery. All nearly always entail an increase of physical capital–labour ratios, the technical composition of capital. This will be reflected in an increase in the organic composition of capital (c/v), in so far as technical advance is neutral between production of means of production and means of consumption.

The production of absolute surplus value could be based on the grim determination of an individual capitalist using lock-outs and dismissals, although class collaboration and state intervention are rarely found wanting when required. In contrast his production of relative surplus value eventually depends critically upon his fellow capitalists, in so far as he himself does not produce the commodities needed to produce the entire wage bundle, making payment in kind. In particular he depends upon other capitalists' accumulation inducing the technical change that brings the value of labour-power down. Why this accumulation takes place and some of its consequences are the subject of Chapter 5.

33

5 Accumulation

THE COERCIVE FORCE OF COMPETITION

In a system of commodity production it is logically possible that the supply and demand for each product would exactly match, with each commodity exchanging at its individual value (the labour-time of production whether it be by the most or least efficient method). Capitalism, however, is dominated by commodity production, and the extension of the market ensures that prices for identical products do not diverge. Even if supply and demand match now, the only way that the owner of a commodity can ensure that it sells at (or above) its individual value is by ensuring that this value is at (or below) the market evaluation. Competition is created between producers in the market. The reaction to this by an independent self-employed artisan, who had survived the vagaries of the market, would be to modify his own output either in quantity or type. These options are also open to the capitalist, but neither is likely to be as effective for his purpose of expanding value as joining in the battle of competition. Marx stressed that this battle is fought by the cheapening of commodities through reducing their value, that is to say the labour-time necessary for their production. This is achieved by technological advance, in particular reaping the fruits of increasing returns to scale interpreted in the widest sense, and this requires accumulation of capital.

Accumulation, from the perspective of an individual capitalist, can be either aggressive or defensive. He can steal an advantage over his rivals by reducing the labour-time of

competitive advertising.) Accumulation is also undertaken by his competitors so that competition itself is reproduced. Competition causes accumulation, accumulation creates competition. Those who fall behind in the accumulation process are destroyed. First it is independent artisans who are swept aside, but later capital turns on itself, big capital destroying little capital as centralisation, credit and concentration amass more and more capital in fewer hands. Accumulation brings frequent technological revolution as the instrument of leaps in productivity. These developments of capital cannot be isolated from the development of the struggle between the two great classes, proletariat and *bourgeoisie*, to which we now turn.

THE DEVELOPMENT OF THE PROLETARIAT

Let us suppose that as capital accumulates the organic composition of capital (c/v) remains unchanged. This does not imply that there is no technological advance, because the relative quantity of physical output may have increased. Provided that the real wage remains unchanged, it follows that the employment of labour increases, since an increased total capital is divided in the same proportions between constant and variable capital.

However, it is unrealistic to expect that the labour supply can be increased indefinitely without an increase in wages. Thus in so far as the wage rate increases faster than productivity in the wage-goods sector there will be a squeeze on profitability. Whilst we have not discussed the quantitative determination of the rate of accumulation it is clear that it will be reduced by a squeeze on profitability. Certainly there will be no accumulation of capital when wages approach such a level that the production of any surplus value at all is threatened. Yet as accumulation slackens so does the demand for labour, and the upward pressure on the wage rate is reduced as labour's power diminishes with unemployment. Profitability is restored, and with it accumulation, and the cycle repeats itself. This argument has to be qualified should the organic composition of capital change. It should be noted that increases in wages are likely to induce a relative substitution of dead for living labour, increasing c/v, but the opposite holds as wages decrease.

This is how Marx characterised the decennial business cycles observed by early nineteenth-century economists. In contrast to them he explained fluctuations in employment by fluctuations in the rate of accumulation and its effects on wages and profitability. He considered absurd the Malthusian doctrine of alternating decimation and stimulation of the size of the proletariat by sexual reproduction in response to wages below and then above subsistence. This could hardly explain ten-year cycles. Marx was also the first economist not to be spellbound by the idea of decreasing returns in agricultural production. In contrast he stressed the productivity of capital.

Described in these aggregate terms, economic activity, generated by changes in the rate of accumulation, appears to fluctuate smoothly. Nothing could be further from the truth. The overall picture may conceal enormous variations between sectors of production and geographical regions within a capitalist economy. Marx highlighted this by pointing to the constant tendency of capital to expel living labour from the production of a given mass of commodities. This tendency exists as long as technological advance is at all labour-saving. But Marx argued that technical change would not only save living labour absolutely, but also relative to other means of production. This was because increases in productivity require increases in the technical composition of capital, since they are achieved by the economies of scale due to factories and machinery. These in themselves increase the technical composition, but they also speed up the process of production. A labourer turns over a given mass of raw materials in a shorter time, reducing the amount of his labour contained in a commodity relative to the other inputs. (Incidentally, it should be noted that these two factors tend to increase the organic composition of capital, provided that the reduction in value of raw materials is not greater than the reduction in value of labour-power.)

The expulsion of living labour from the production of a

given mass of commodities may be accompanied by an overall expansion in employment with the aggregate expansion of production. Competitive accumulation, however, proceeds in an unco-ordinated fashion. Across sectors and regions outputs and employment will not expand in balanced proportions. With the technological changes there will now be a shortage now an excess of labour available, but with the expulsion of living labour from the labour process, there will be a continuous flow of labour into unemployment to form a surplus population, or what Marx called an industrial reserve army of unemployed. Among these will be created a layer of permanently unemployed, condemned to relative pauperisation by their relative unsuitability for capitalist employment, whether it be because of age, discrimination, or physical or mental disability. The greater is the reserve army relative to employment, the greater is the competition for employment and the lower will be wages. But the greater is the absolute size of the reserve army and its layer of permanently unemployed, the greater is the extension of poverty and misery. Marx singled out this feature of capitalism as the absolute general law of capitalist accumulation.

So far we have analysed the requirements that capital accumulation places on the proletariat – a constant disruption of individual and social life. Particular changes may be forced by political, economic and legal coercion, or induced by wage increases. The particular method chosen and the outcome will depend upon the strength of organisation behind the two classes. Under capitalism, as for any mode of production, the ruling class finds its strength in all superstructural phenomena, the state, the law, and not least the political and ideological consciousness generated by the notions of economic and political freedom. In addition the *bourgeoisie*'s strength increases as accumulation is accompanied by greater centralisation. However, at the same time as capital is centralised, so are masses of workers concentrated together in the organisation of production. Their social organisation in production encourages their political and economic organisation. As misery and oppression are extended with unemployment, so grows the strength, material conditions, organisation and discipline of the proletariat with the development of its material conditions. Capitalism fulfils the positive role of developing society's productive potential. Yet at the same time it develops both the agent of its own destruction – an organised proletariat – and the rationale for that destruction: the socialisation of consumption to be accomplished by a socially co-ordinated plan harnessing that productive potential. The proletariat accomplishes its historical role, expropriation of the *bourgeoisie* when *bourgeois* society can no longer provide the conditions that both capital and labour require of it. The economic conditions under which this may occur are discussed in Chapter 8.

6 The Transition to Capitalism

So far we have characterised capitalism as a mode of production and revealed the logic and consequences of its compulsion toward accumulation. This provides us with a framework in which the development of capitalism as the world's dominant mode of production can be understood. For, having uncovered the relations of production specific to capitalism, we can isolate the forces behind their creation from the mass of phenomena peculiar to *bourgeois* revolution. Marx devoted a large section of Volume I of *Capital* to the task of interpreting the genesis of British capitalism, and this must stand as a major application and confirmation of his conception of historical change. Here we can only outline the theoretical aspects of his work, and refer the reader to *Capital* and later Marxists for more concrete study of the causes of the nature, timing and location of the first industrial revolution.

The essential feature of capitalism is the existence of labour-power as a commodity. A necessary condition for this is the separation of labour from ownership or claim to the means of production. The labourer has to depend upon somebody else to provide these, otherwise he would sell the product of his day's labour rather than his labouring day. On the other side of the coin must be the capitalist with money to advance to purchase labour-power and maintain ownership of the other means of production. The establishment of these social relations of production out of feudalist ones holds the key to the birth of capitalism.

41

In any society beyond the most primitive there will be saving of produce to form means of production for the future, whether it be hunting weapon, corn seed, animal stock or machinery. Capitalism is distinguished by the rate of increase of saving that is made. Marx found it commonplace, once capitalism had been established, for other economists to place its creation at the hands of self-sacrificing and energetic entrepreneurs, ploughing back their meagre profits into their businesses. More recently development economists have tended to consider low rates of saving as a major barrier to industrialisation. Marx poured scorn on such a limited outlook. Capitalism was founded on the forcible separation of labour from the existing means of production, and not the capitalisation of surplus value that characterises developed capitalism. This entailed the conversion of the use of existing means of production, including labour-power, into their social use in capitalistic organisation. This does not require in the first instance any additional accumulation of means of production or even their more efficient use, just their operation according to new relations. Once this has occurred the process of competitive accumulation gathers its own momentum.

Since the dominant sector of production in the pre-capitalist era was agriculture, this sector contained the source of a class of 'free' wage-labourers. The secret of primitive or early accumulation of capital lay then in the history of the expropriation of the agricultural population from the land, the destruction of the right or custom of individual independent cultivation (even if feudal dues need be paid). This could be undertaken on an individual basis by landowners responding to the growing claims of exchange criteria, but required the power of the state to make any headway in a violent and violently resisted process. The state's intervention, representing the interests of an emerging *bourgeoisie*, was twofold. First enclosure movements dispossessed the peasantry of both common and individual land usage. The landless labourer was created. Secondly wage legislation and systems of social security, culminating in the Poor Law of 1834, forced long hours and discipline on the landless labourer. This turned the landless into a wage labourer, creating the source of absolute surplus value.

42

Here we cannot stress too strongly Marx's emphasis on the conversion of the method of use of the existing means of production rather than their explosive accumulation. No doubt technical progress and reorganisation of production contributed to the rise in agricultural output that was to feed an industrial proletariat. Few labourers felt the gain of this increased output, and for those that did, it must have paled into insignificance against the deterioration of working conditions and the destruction of a way of life. Illustrative of this is the necessity of physical force in the creation of the proletariat rather than the smooth operation of market forces. This contrasts with most present-day labour relations, where the dull compulsion of economic relations and their development through tradition, education and habit induces the working class to look upon the conditions of the capitalist mode of production as self-evident. Force is rarely used now, because labour is effectively tied to capital and appears as if it always has been and always will be.

The capitalist first appears as a farmer and is long in embryonic form. In Britain he came to the fore through the coincidence of favourable economic conditions – the discovery and hoarding of precious metals, and low rent and wages. The industrial capitalist's genesis was less protracted. He developed more out of artisans and guilds depending upon the absorption of the labourers that capitalistic farming pushed out. Simultaneously a domestic market was created for the produce of industrial capital by the ending of the peasantry's essentially self-sufficient livelihood. Previously they had been able to serve their own needs, means of production being made available according to feudal custom. With the advent of capitalism, money to advance to purchase means of production is required to pursue independent production. Thus it is not necessarily the efficiency of capital that destroys household production: indeed, household production still persisted in sweat shops. The technical methods of production remain unchanged, but the partial control of output and access to inputs is lost to the producers.

This extremely brief account explains the origins of the capitalist relations of production. By the seventeenth century the first enclosure movement (another was to follow in the eighteenth century) had been completed, creating a landless labouring class. In the eighteenth century the use of the national debt, the taxation system, the protectionist system, and the exploitation of colonies to accumulate wealth had reached its climax. The combination of labour and wealth in capitalist relations accompanied these processes, with the nineteenth century heralding the technological innovation and growth of industrial society.

THE CIRCUIT AS A WHOLE

The circuit of industrial capital is best represented by a circular flow diagram. As the circuit repeats itself, surplus value (m) is thrown off. This shows that capital as self-expanding value embraces not only definite social relations of production, but is also a circular movement going through its various stages. If m is accumulated for use as capital we could think of extended reproduction as being represented by an outward spiral movement.

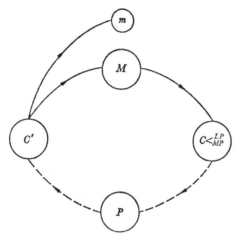

FIG. 3. Circuit of capital

Industrial capital changes successively into its three forms: money capital (M), productive capital (P), and commodity capital (C'). Each form presupposes the existence of the other forms because it presupposes the circuit itself. This allows us to distinguish the function of each of the forms of capital from its function as capital. In societies where they exist, money, factor inputs, and commodities can always function as means of payment, means of production, and a depository of exchange value respectively, but they only act as capital when they follow these functions in the circuit of capital. Then, money-capital acts as a means of purchasing labour-power, productive capital acts as means of producing surplus value, and commodity-capital acts as the depository of surplus value.

47

In the movement through the circuit we can identify two spheres of activity: production and circulation. The sphere of production lies between C and C'. It was Marx's abstraction to define all value as being added in the sphere of production by living labour which also preserved the value of constant capital. This has profound implications for his theory of distribution because it explains what it is he is describing as being distributed. The sphere of circulation contains the process of exchange between C' and C. Even if capital and labour are used in the exchange process they add no value to output!

This assumption seems strange to orthodox economists because they are usually interested in obtaining a price theory by aggregating factors used in production and exchange. But Marx was interested in the social relations of distribution, and in particular the method of distributing value as he defined it, since this would reveal the likely role to be played by income recipients in class struggle. Thus, whilst commercial capital adds no value, this does not prevent its receiving a share of value according to the appropriate distributional relations which characterise capitalism (see Chapter 9).

When we have constructed the circuit of capital in circular form, we see that it becomes arbitrary to open and close the circuit with money capital, just as a circle has no beginning or end. Note that the money circuit contains the interruption of the sphere of circulation by the sphere of production. In characterising capital as self-expanding value we found that the capitalist's motive was to buy in order to sell dearer. So, for capital seen from the perspective of the money circuit, production appears as a necessary but unfortunate interruption in the process of money-making. Merchants' capital can avoid this interruption, although it depends upon production elsewhere, but industrial capital cannot. If a nation's capital is seized by the attempt to make profit without the unavoidable link of production, it may find itself in a speculative boom which eventually crashes when the economy is brought back to the reality of the need for production.

Marx also analysed the circuit from two other perspectives, from productive capital and from commodity-capital. The circuit of productive capital begins and ends with P, production, and so the purpose of the circuit appears to be production, and, in so far as surplus value is accumulated, production on an extended scale. In contrast to the money circuit, for the productive circuit, the sphere of circulation appears as a necessary but unwanted intervention in the sphere of production. Economists more often than capitalists tend to ignore this necessary mediation by exchange, and we can cite neo-classical and von Neumann growth theory in this context. Nevertheless a capitalist who unwittingly or otherwise produces a growing inventory of commodities with the expectation or hope of sale is soon brought back to reality with the loss of his working capital. It is not sufficient to produce (surplus) value, it has to be realised.

The circuit of commodity-capital begins and ends with C', and so the purpose of the circuit appears to be to generate consumption. As the sphere of circulation is followed by the sphere of production, neither sphere is interrupted by the other, so neither appears as evil or unnecessary. Capital, seen from this perspective, is reflected in neo-classical general equilibrium theory, where the neo-classical theories of production and exchange are integrated. It also leads to the popular myth that the purpose of production is consumption (and so not profit or exchange).

We have described the three circuits of capital which together form the circuit as a whole. One might wonder why there are not four circuits of capital, with each 'node' on the circuit $(P, C', M$ and $C)$ forming a starting and finishing point. The reason why $C <^{LP}_{MP}$ is not the basis for a circuit of capital is that the C is not capital. The means of production purchased in this C may be another capitalist's commodity production and hence commodity-capital. However, labour-power is never capital until it is purchased, and then it becomes productive capital and not commodity-capital, which must contain produced surplus value. Thus, whilst from a technical point of view capitalism can be self-reliant for raw materials, it depends upon the social reproduction of labour-power from outside the pure system of production. This entails the use of political, ideological and legal as well as economic power.

The point is to get the labourer to work. The same problems do not exist in getting a machine to work.

As we have hinted above, views of capital's process of reproduction corresponding to each circuit of capital can be constructed. These need not be uncritical of capitalism, but individually they are always inadequate, stressing one or more of the processes of production, consumption, exchange, profit-making and accumulation at the expense of the others. Only fleetingly, as they enter the circuit, do labour-power and produced means of production appear separated and then, not forming capital, they do not generate a view of the circuit as a whole. As a result orthodox economic theories can eliminate class relations altogether. Where they do enter it is inevitably in distributional relations (the effect on the consumption function) and not those of production.

The money circuit suggests models of exchange. For the economy the matching of supply and demand becomes the be all and end all. Capital and labour are merely seen as productive services, either in full employment or a Keynesian unemployment equilibrium. Difficulties are merely associated with the informational services performed by the price (and interest rate) mechanism. The productive circuit attempts to ignore the market. This yields an excellent input–output theory for a planned economy, but this bears faint resemblance to capitalism. The commodity circuit sees the harmonious interaction of the purpose, consumption, and of the means, production. It is the strength of Marx's circuit of capital to expose the limitations of these outlooks. At the same time it reveals the functions of the forms in which capital appears and constructs a basis on which major economic categories and phenomena can be understood.

8 Crises

THE NATURE OF CRISES

Capitalism will be in or on the verge of a crisis whenever the social accumulation of capital is interrupted. In such a circumstance the working class will be posed with two alternatives. It may concede an economic, political or social defeat to restore capital to its normal condition of reproduction on an extended scale. This could, for example, involve a fall in wages or employment, the fighting of a war, or an upheaval in working conditions. Alternatively the working class can overthrow the system of capitalist production. Marx believed that crises were endemic to capitalism, and in this sense alone revolution against capitalism was inevitable. For, again and again, the working class would take defeat, but with the lesson of defeat and its growing strength and organisation, defeat would eventually be inflicted on the *bourgeoisie* at the hands of the proletariat.

Marx's theory of the inevitability of crises depends upon his law of the tendency of the rate of profit to fall. This law will be discussed in the following section. For the moment it should be observed that crises in capitalism can occur apart from movements in the rate of profit and indeed from outside the pure circuit of capital, with social upheaval not directly economic in character. However, for capitalism, in contrast to other modes of production, these extraneous factors (such as war, natural disaster, or political instability) are rarely the causes of economic crises but are more likely to be consequences. This is because of capital's high development of

51

the productive forces, which brings with it power over nature and economic control of civil society. On the other hand this means that the cause of crises must be placed in the economic system and not in 'random' events.

Marx emphasised that crises could always arise because of the contradiction between the production of social use-values and their individual or, more exactly, private consumption. It is only under capitalism, where production for exchange rather than use dominates, that overproduction of a commodity can prove an embarrassment. Elsewhere it would be a cause for celebration, because it would mean increased consumption. But for capital consumption is not enough, profit must be realised as well. This depends upon sale, and if this becomes impossible production may be curtailed and capital operate on a reduced scale. This applies to a single set of capitalists producing a particular commodity. They may have been subject to some disturbance generated within the economic sphere (see Chapter 5) or elsewhere. However, it must not be forgotten that the reproduction of their capitals on an extended scale is intimately integrated with other circuits of capital. Their demands for inputs may be another capitalist's supply and vice versa and so on to other capitalists. The economy may be seen as a system of expanding circuits linked together like interlocking cog-wheels. If one set of wheels grinds to a halt or slows down, so may others throughout the system. It is the necessary but unplanned interlocking of capitals that led Marx to talk of the anarchy of capitalist production.

What we have been examining is the breakdown of an individual capitalist's circuit of capital and the possible social consequences given private decisions on production and purchase. We pursue this further on the assumption that commodities exchange at their values. A circuit of capital may be broken in any of its links (see Fig. 3 in Chapter 7). The break may be either voluntary or involuntary on the part of the capitalist. He may be either unwilling but able or willing but unable to allow the circuit to continue. In the first case the capitalist will be speculating. Either he anticipates that profitability may be increased by delaying the circuit, or he may hope to create or exploit a monopoly position by doing so.

52

In the second case the capitalist is subject to forces beyond his control.

There is unlikely to be a break of the circuit in the sphere of production provided labour honours its contract and there are no technical or natural disasters. Thus almost all crises will appear to originate in the sphere of circulation as an inability or unwillingness to buy or sell. Consider the arm $M-C <^{LP}_{MP}$. A voluntary break here implies that C could be bought, but the owner of the M presumably anticipates a lower price for his inputs or hopes to create such a lower price. In particular, for the labour input, he may do this by imposing a lock-out. On the other hand the break in the circuit could be involuntary. The owners of the inputs may attempt to create or exploit a monopoly position – in particular labour may strike. Alternatively inputs may not be available because, in the previous round of social production, outputs – partly present inputs – may have been produced in the wrong proportions. This will provide for an excess demand of a particular commodity and necessarily an excess supply in some other sector. If this situation becomes generalised across many producers we may describe the situation as a crisis of disproportionality. These remarks need to be modified if the commodity in short supply is labour-power. Then there will be an excess demand for labour but also an excess supply of unused money-capital.

A break in the sphere of circulation may also appear between C' and M. A capitalist may speculate about the future price of his commodity-capital in case of a voluntary break. Alternatively he may be unable to sell his produce. This means his commodity is in excess supply. This could be because of a disproportionality (see previous paragraph), or alternatively those who normally buy his commodity may be unable to do so because they do not have money to hand. If other circuits have been broken, for whatever reason, workers, capitalists and others will not receive their regular flow of money income and hence will not make a regular flow of money expenditures. If this last situation becomes generalised we talk of a crisis of underconsumption.

Marxists have usually looked at crises of underconsumption

and disproportionality by dividing the economy into two sectors, investment and consumption, following Marx's scheme for extended reproduction (not covered in this book). Some have argued that there is a persistent tendency for the supply of consumption goods to outstrip the demand for them, others that the tendency exists for a disproportionately large production of investment goods. Both are logically possible, but disproportions – overproduction in one sector underproduction in another – are just as likely to occur within the consumption and investment goods sectors as between the two as aggregates. In all this it is possible to confuse a crisis of disproportionality, in which consumption goods are in excess supply, with a crisis of underconsumption. This last will be characterised by a general overproduction of commodities and excess capacity and must be generated by some 'exogenous' disturbance. A crisis of disproportionality does not presuppose such an 'exogenous' disturbance but may be one, tending to generate a crisis of underconsumption.

Breaks in individual circuits of capital will occur infinitely often given the anarchy of capitalist production, fluctuations in market prices, the vagaries of the credit system, speculation, monopolisation, and the economic obsolescence of fixed capital with technological progress. Occasionally a crisis will be generated, its extent depending upon the pattern of adjustment in disequilibrium. This is nothing more or less than a Keynesian analysis of the multiplier, yielding an unemployment equilibrium for underconsumption and a 'bottleneck' disequilibrium for disproportionality. It describes and demonstrates the possibility of crises. It leaves aside the motive of capitalist production: profit. The most important factor from the capitalist's standpoint is the amount of profit thrown off by the circuit of capital. All obstacles to the circuit's movement may be overcome if m is large enough. Should profitability be improving capitalists will be reluctant to speculate, deny wage increases, or in any way hinder the process of money-making. Crises will not be generated. In the last analysis a potential cause of a crisis is more than likely to be insignificant, given sufficient profitability. Profits can pay and pave the way.

54

However, should profitability be falling, then not only will some capitalists be expelled from production by bankruptcy, but general pessimism will reign, production will be curtailed, and a crisis will be generated. Movements in profitability depend upon movements in values. But, as we have seen, the process of competitive accumulation brings frequent reductions in the values of all commodities. It is a contradictory feature of capital that individual profit is pursued by reducing values through relative expulsion of living labour, which is the source of surplus value, from production. Thus accumulation in pursuit of profitability may prove unsuccessful.

THE LAW OF THE TENDENCY OF THE RATE OF PROFIT TO FALL

In general the classical economists believed that capitalism was burdened with an unavoidable law: a tendency for the rate of profit to fall to a level at which accumulation would cease and wages decline to subsistence levels. When this situation was reached the economy was said to be in a stationary state. Such theories were always based on the belief in the existence of diminishing returns to land. Mill, for example, argued that but for this physical property all the laws of political economy would be different.

Whilst Marx himself constructed a theory to explain the tendency of the rate of profit to fall, he placed it entirely in the context of capitalist production and did not refer to agriculture specifically at all. Indeed his arguments depend upon increasing returns to scale in capitalist production as opposed to decreasing returns to scale in agriculture. Before embarking on an assessment of Marx's theory, it should be noted that his contribution on this is often ambiguous and confusing. This may be because Volume III, like Volume II, of *Capital* was never finally prepared for publication. In any case the reader should be warned that this is a highly controversial area.

In its simplest form Marx's argument is as follows. The average rate of profit $r = S/(C+V)$, where S is total surplus produced and $C + V$ is total (constant and variable) capital advanced

$$r = \frac{S/V}{C/V + 1} = \frac{e}{d + 1}$$

where e is the rate of exploitation and d the social organic composition of capital. Now it has already been argued that, as a consequence of accumulation, d tends to rise and hence, if e remains unchanged, r must fall.

It is important to recall why d should rise. It is because competitive accumulation in pursuit of economies of scale and reduced values is realised by increases in fixed capital and faster man-use of constant capital. That accumulation and the falling rate of profit are linked together by a rising organic composition of capital means that, despite the relative expulsion of living labour from production and the lack of surplus value relative to capital advanced, there is but for exceptional circumstances an absolute increase in both surplus value and employment. Thus whilst the rate of profit and labour–capital ratio fall, profits and employment rise.

Marx modified this argument to take account of what he called counteracting influences, borrowing this term (and some analysis) from Mill's *Principles of Political Economy*. Note first that if some large portion of capital takes a low rate of return, then the general average may be *ceteris paribus* increased. Marx cited the railway companies, and more recently some nationalised industries may be seen in this light. Secondly any factor which tends to enhance profitability also encourages a renewal of accumulation on an even larger scale, possibly bringing heavier pressure to bear on the rate of profit.

The counteracting influences can be divided into two types: those that temper the rise in the organic composition and those that raise the rate of exploitation. Of the former there is the cheapening of material inputs relative to wage-goods, whether by foreign trade – particularly exploitation of colonies – or by bias in technological advance. Also the expansion of capital into non-capitalist areas can relieve competitive pressure by the creation or capture of markets formerly served by other modes of production.

The rise in the rate of exploitation which can occur with accumulation is clearly anticipated by Marx to be insufficient to offset the effect on the rate of profit of the increase in the organic composition of capital. e may be increased by the production of absolute or relative surplus value. The former contains limited scope, but the latter positively accompanies accumulation, as the wage-goods decrease in value along with other commodities. On the other hand accumulation, which is the means of reducing value, simultaneously increases the absolute demand for labour, strengthening its bargaining position and creating the possibility of higher wages. Given the length of the working day is fixed, it is easy to see that wages must rise, even if their value falls, if the rate of profit is to fall. For otherwise individual capitalists could continue to operate without loss of profitability with their existing scale and method of production and possibly improve profitability by operating with some new (larger) scale or method.

Marx's theory can be illustrated by considering a special case. Suppose that large-scale production involves an increase in the physical capital required to produce a commodity, but that its labour-time of production is reduced over small-scale production by a more than compensating decrease in the living labour-time required for production. (For example, consider handicraft and factory production of chairs.) Here the largest capital is placed best competitively, this induces accumulation by all capitalists, and the consequences are an increase in the organic composition of capital, reduction in the value of commodities, absolute expulsion of living labour from the production of commodities, but possibly absolute increase in the labour force. Whilst wages and the rate of surplus value rise, the rate of profit can fall as the organic composition of capital increases enormously.

From this discussion it becomes clear that it would be nonsense to hypothesise a long-run tendency of the rate of profit to fall in the sense that over a period of one hundred years the rate of profit must have become lower. This is because technological advance and the introduction of new processes can allow simultaneous increases in the rate of profit and wages. Also, if a drop in profitability brings on a

57

crisis, so the renewal of capitalist accumulation consequently requires a restoration of profitability, possibly at a higher level than that existing previously. This can be accomplished by reorganisation of the economy in the widest sense and, if necessary, by wage reductions.

The tendency of the rate of profit to fall can only be seen, as Marx implicitly described it in Volume I, as underlying the business cycle. Its force is felt when counteracting influences no longer prove strong enough – this depending upon a complex of factors embracing technological, political and other conditions. Only in this sense can a falling rate of profit be considered a logical necessity. Mathematically a theoretical demonstration of its possible fall can be given, but its actual fall rests on the relative strength at particular times of the trends identified by Marx. The anarchy of capitalist production makes crises possible, but a falling rate of profit makes them inevitable. This is because a crisis is the social outcome of the interaction of pessimistic capitalists' individual decisions, whereas a falling rate of profit is a social outcome that makes those decisions certain.

9 Notes on Theory of Distribution

WAGES AND PROFITS

Marx's theory of value is based on labour-time expended in the sphere of production. His theory of distribution is concerned with analysing the way or relationships by which value is distributed in society, and this chapter considers some of these distributional relationships. Clearly the distribution theory presupposes the value theory, but it should not be confused with a price theory. Rather the relations of distribution can be thought of as a framework which explains the sources of income under capitalism, and in which the quantitative distribution of income to those sources may be studied. In contrast a price theory would depend upon the factors determining supply and demand. These are exhaustively described by orthodox theory, but the description reveals few secrets. In this case they can only be uncovered by examining the relations of distribution and their development. These in turn depend upon the development of the relationship between the relations of and forces of production.

The most important distributional relationship studied by Marx is that based on the pure system of capitalist production: the wage (and profit) system. This is treated throughout all volumes of *Capital*, whereas other distributional relations were confined to and almost filled Volume III. This relationship is quantified by the rate of surplus value, even though wage payments may take varied forms such as piece and time wages,

59

'profit-sharing', overtime and so on. The rate of exploitation depends in the last analysis on class struggle in the economic sphere, that is to say conflict over wages and the length and conditions of the working day, the outcome being decided by relative class strength and organisation. This gives the quantitative distribution of value between capital and labour an historical element, which itself determines the individual characteristics of utility and skills so much stressed by orthodox neo-classical economists. The economic struggle between capital and labour cannot be understood independently of the development of education, the family, and the state – as well as trade-union strength, monopoly power, and the rate of accumulation. On the other hand struggle within the wage system cannot by itself bring down capitalism. For if it is pursued beyond the point where accumulation has collapsed workers cannot help but be aware of the consequences of their action, and wage demands will pale into insignificance against more fundamental threats to the capitalist relations of production. Workers are faced with the choice: either moderate wage claims, or investment slackens with falling employment. This is the conventional wisdom, and the consciousness necessary to reject this wisdom requires the wisdom to reject capitalism. In other words the wage-system poses strict historical limits on the level of wages. Challenging those limits can never be a purely economic struggle.

Exactly the same sort of factors that affect the distribution between capital and labour influence the relative distribution between wage-earners. Beyond reducing skilled labour to units of unskilled labour, Marx gave only scattered remarks about wage differentials. In theory, with a given rate of exploitation, workers would be remunerated according to their contribution of unskilled labour units. In practice the rate of exploitation varies with ethnic, age, sex, regional, craft, sectoral and organisational differences. These factors can only be seriously studied in an historical context and cannot be taken for granted.

The distribution of profits between capitalists was treated at great length by Marx mainly because it posed an apparent inconsistency in the labour theory of value, which had puzzled the classical economists. Ricardo, with some hindsight, might have argued as follows. An entrepreneur advances capital $c+v$ by which surplus value s is created and value $c+v+s$ is realised. Provided commodities sell at their values the rate of profit for the entrepreneur will be

$$r = \frac{s}{c+v} = \frac{e}{c/v+1}$$

For factor mobility, e and r will be equalised across the economy by competition. From this it follows that c/v must be the same in every firm. However, technical differences between sectors must allow for great varieties of c/v in the economy. The assumption that commodities exchange at their values must be dropped. Indeed those commodities produced with a relatively high (low) c/v must have a relatively higher (lower) price than their value. Only some commodity of 'average' c/v will exchange at its value.

Marx came to the same sort of conclusions as this, for he had only assumed that commodities exchanged at their value for simplicity. He criticised the classical economists for expecting the labour theory of value, a theory of production, to explain relations of distribution. They assumed that wages, prices and profits existed without explaining them and their dependence on capitalist production. Profit exists because of the particular social relations of production peculiar to capitalism. The relation under which profit is distributed is not according to how much surplus value is produced in each firm, but by how much money-capital is advanced by each entrepreneur.

At any one time there will be a social aggregate of capital advanced $(C+V)$ and produced surplus value (S). S will be shared among entrepreneurs according to their share of $C+V$. The share of surplus per unit of advanced capital will be given by the general rate of profit $S/(C+V) = r$. Now an individual capitalist whose cost of production is $c+v$ receives a surplus $(c+v)r$ and must sell at a modified value or price of production $(c+v)(1+r)$ to realise his cost and share of surplus. This modified value will only equal $c+v+s$ if $c/v = C/V$. It is clear that Marx is using the actual average C/V in the economy to determine modified values. This is not a strictly correct procedure for, as Marx observed, this average commodity may not itself exchange at its value.

The 'correct' solution of the transformation of values into prices requires fairly sophisticated linear algebra to find the appropriate average commodity, and is not reproduced here. Suffice it to remark that the solution is not so important as the social analysis behind it. Marx saw the rate of profit as the monetary expression of the existence of exploitation and the accounting mechanism by which surplus value is distributed. The rate of profit is readily observed, but exploitation and surplus value are not. His critique of the classical school seems relatively trivial to present-day economists, including some who solve the transformation problem 'correctly'. For them prices and the rate of profit are technically determined given the level of wages. It has become obvious that in a market economy prices must be equalised by factor mobility, and profitability depends upon all the techniques of production. The classical economists, in so far as they clung to a labour theory of value, were attempting to resolve the contradiction of the production of value by labour and its distribution by capital. Present-day economists have not solved this contradiction, but have ignored its first component.

MERCHANTS' CAPITAL

In the next three sections we examine merchants' capital, interest-bearing capital, and rent of land to discover the manner in which value is distributed and the modifications that need to be made to the analysis of industrial capital in its pure form. For simplicity we treat each independently of the others.

Merchants' capital is simply capital functioning in the sphere of circulation. It can take two forms: commercial capital used for exchange within a currency area and money-dealing capital used in exchange between currency areas for foreign trade. Here we concentrate on commercial capital, and in addition ignore speculation.

Whilst merchants' capital is dependent upon production as part of the circuit of capital, the converse is not true. The industrial capitalist in theory does not need the merchant and will not use him unless this allows an economy in time or money cost in selling. Nevertheless merchants' capital has a certain external independence of industrial capital, with its ability to roam over many products and continue activity in the sphere of circulation when the sphere of production has been interrupted. If this external independence over-reaches itself, however, the internal dependence on production is likely to be restored by a crisis of some sort.

Although merchants' capital may be expended on (exploited) labour and other means of production as well as on commodities, because it only operates in the sphere of circulation, it adds no value and so no surplus value to commodities. In the sphere of circulation surplus value is only realised, this being possible because it has already been produced in the sphere of production. Merchants' capital can only be considered to produce surplus value indirectly by reducing the costs of circulation and so allowing more capital to be advanced as industrial capital.

Although commercial capital creates no surplus value it must appropriate some, otherwise it would not be advanced. Commercial capital receives surplus value in an identical way to any industrial capital: according to share'of capital advanced. Suppose that the costs of circulation are purely monetary, and that commercial capital used in aggregate is M. Total surplus value (S) must then be shared between an aggregate capital $C + V + M$ yielding a general rate of profit $S/(C + V + M)$. An industrial capitalist's cost of production remains at $c + v$, and his selling price to merchants is $(c + v)(1 + r)$. The merchant's selling price is $(c + v)(1 + r) + mr$, as he adds commercial profit to his cost price, where m is the average money he requires to circulate a commodity. On average this equals $c + v + s$, by definition of r. Thus industrial capitalists sell at below value to merchants who sell at value, the difference forming commercial profit.

More generally merchants have material costs of production K, financing commercial labourers and their offices. These costs (K) form not only a part of aggregate advanced capital, but also drain on the surplus value (S) to be distributed. The rate of profit becomes

$$r = \frac{S - K}{C + V + M + K}$$

K being financed out of surplus value. Industrial capital's cost and selling price are respectively $(c + v)$ and $(c + v)(1 + r)$. Merchants' selling price is $(c + v)(1 + r) + mr + k(1 + r)$. Again on average this is exactly equal to value by definition of r. Industrial capitalists sell below value to merchants who sell at value, the difference forming commercial profit and expenses, both appropriating surplus value, rather than adding to it.

Thus we find that merchants' capital feeds parasitically off industrial capital, but simultaneously can stimulate its growth by reducing the costs of circulation. Industrial and merchant capitalists have a joint interest in raising the rate of surplus value, as this raises the rate of profit and remuneration for both. Further the action of merchants' capital in no way impairs the general analysis of capital in its pure industrial circuit, since the assumption that commodities exchange at that value remains a legitimate abstraction.

INTEREST-BEARING CAPITAL

Interest-bearing capital arises whenever one capitalist lends money to another to employ as capital. In this instance capital becomes a commodity, but it is not commodity-capital since this always contains produced surplus value. It is capital as a commodity, not industrial capital in commodity form, and because as such interest-bearing capital must have a use-value and an exchange-value its use-value is its ability to expand value. This is the property that the borrower purchases and which he uses to produce average profit. The price he pays for this privilege is the rate of interest.

Marx argued that, although the rate of interest can be considered to be the price of the commodity capital, unlike other commodities, the quantitative determination of the rate of interest cannot be based on labour-time. In contrast it is determined by competition, which does not merely perform the function of smoothing away deviations between rates. Presumably Marx meant that the rate of interest depends upon conditions of supply and demand, that subjective factors would permanently enter into its determination. First find those who are able to be capitalists, that is to say those who are sufficiently wealthy not to be bound by work; discover also those who wish to be 'coupon-clippers' and lead the aristocratic life, rather than be active entrepreneurs. Then the prevailing institutional (financial), technical (price of luxuries) and business (expectations) conditions will bring about a rate of interest through competition which will equate the supply of and demand for money-capital. Thus whilst Marx viewed competition as determining the rate of interest, he vehemently attacked the classical notion of a natural rate, analogous to the natural price of a commodity determined by labour-time and independent of distribution.

When interest-bearing capital is used for industrial production, before the industrial circuit of capital begins, money has to be borrowed. After the circuit has been completed money must be returned to the lender in quantity over and above his initial outlay. This does not mean that the entire surplus value produced is appropriated by the lender or financier. Part of it will be retained by the industrial capitalist or entrepreneur. Thus the rate of profit (r) can be divided into two parts, the rate of interest (i) and the rate of profit of enterprise (f), where $r = f + i$. Now the direct determination of r and prices by the rate of exploitation and values in production remains unaltered by the existence of interest-bearing capital. It only alters the distribution of surplus value allowing the financier his share according to competition for money-capital. We see that financier and entrepreneur have a common interest in raising the rate of exploitation, but a conflict in the division of a given quantity of surplus value. The financier divorced from ownership and control of the production process, can nevertheless consider his money and his abstinence as the source of profit for both. He sees the entrepreneur in the

65

same light as the entrepreneur sees the workers and other means of production. The entrepreneur, in contrast, believes his skills of organisation produces the dividends he has to share with the parasitic financier.

RENT OF LAND

In his theory of rent Ricardo assumed that equal quantities of capital and labour are applied to lands of different quality. He deduced that the price of corn is determined by the labour-time of production of corn on the worst (marginal) land in use. In addition, rent accruing to the owners of superior land equals the difference in value between the produce on that land and the produce on an equal quantity of the worst land. The worst land in use carried no rent. Ricardo was interested in the extensive margin and in particular the distribution of income as agricultural production was forced on to inferior land. This created increasing rent in corn and value for landlords as production expanded, but reduced the corn and value available per unit of capital and labour because of the diminishing returns to land. Marx described the rent produced in Ricardo's theory by the extensive margin by the term Differential Rent I, but not surprisingly, in view of his estimate of the productive power of capital, he also studied the intensive margin. This concerns the increased productivity of land which is due to the application of different quantities of capital and labour on lands of different quality. What is important now, for a theory of differential rent, is not the worst land in use but the worst production process in use, that is to say the most expensive in terms of labour-time. This might not be the worst land in use if more capital and labour are applied to a superior land. In this case Marx spoke of Differential Rent II, for which, *contra* Ricardo, rent might be paid on the worst land.

Neoclassical economists should be familiar with this sort of argument. They are simply marginal productivity determinations of the value of rent. Indeed Jevons was to argue that Ricardo's theory of rent contained the essence of all distribution theory. However, Marx was far from satisfied with extending Ricardo's theory of differential rent to the intensive margin to take account of the marginal physical product of capital and labour as well as of land. He argued that even if some land were not in use and it were all of the same quality, rent would be paid because of the absolute monopoly of landed-property by the landowning class. Together capitalists' and landowners' respective monopoly ownership of the produced and natural means of production ties the labourer to exploitation, since he cannot become an independent producer. However, the landowner's ownership of landed property also forms a barrier to the capitalist's pursuit of surplus value in so far as that landed property is monopolised and essential for production, for example particularly in the case of agricultural production. The price to capital of breaking down this barrier is rent. To distinguish this form of rent, created alone by the monopoly of landed property, from differential rent, Marx called it absolute rent. Its quantity is determined by the power of landlords *vis-à-vis* capitalists.

With differential rent the price of a commodity will depend upon the labour-time of production at the margin. This will have no systematic relation to the value of the commodity based on its average time of production on all lands. Landlords will appropriate surplus value according to the superiority of their land over the margin. For absolute rent the price of a commodity will not even bear any relation to the labour-time of production at the margin. Commodities which are land-intensive in production will be more expensive according to absolute rent paid. Both forms of rent form a subtraction from the surplus value to be distributed to capital.

In the case of differential rent landowners have no direct interest in the distributional struggle between labour and capital. In so far as increases in wages increase demand for their produce and consequently their land, they might side with the proletariat. On the other hand, for absolute rent, landowners are more likely to ally with the *bourgeoisie* against the proletariat in order to extract a greater surplus value to be shared by raising the rate of exploitation. Alternatively they could possibly side with the proletariat against the *bourgeoisie*, their hope being a greater share of surplus value. To the individual capitalist rent of land is likely to resemble the cost of any other means of production. The social relations behind its formation will be lost in the act of reducing costs and creating profits, just as labour is treated like other inputs for these purposes. Finally note that we have analysed rent from the perspective of agricultural production. Any other monopoly of natural means of production, for example mines, would be studied similarly.

DISTRIBUTIONAL AND CLASS RELATIONS

Wages, profits and rent are the major economic categories by which value is distributed after due allowance is made for the replacement cost of constant capital. To these revenues and their sources – labour, capital and land – correspond the three great classes in society: proletariat, *bourgeoisie* and land-owners. We have examined how these classes relate to each other and the means of production and the implications of this for distributional relations.

Here we cannot develop Marx's theory of class structure at length, but a few notes are necessary. The first stage in distinguishing classes is always the identification of the relations of production peculiar to the dominant mode of production prevailing. This yields a ruling class and the ruled: the non-workers and workers, oppressors and oppressed. However, in any particular society or historical phase, this simple dichotomy may always be complicated in either of two ways. First the remnants of classes from previous modes of production may exist and so may the emerging classes of a future mode. These are transitional classes owning their existence to the passage of society from one mode of production to another, for example peasantry and landlords under capitalism and *bourgeoisie* and proletariat under feudalism. Secondly there may arise classes specific to the dominant mode of production, but which do not fall into the basic dichotomy. These may be distinguished by their particular relations to the means of production and their political interests and organisations. Under capitalism these

68

interests are invariably economic, that is to say distributional, and we can cite the *petit-bourgeoisie* and independent producers as examples. These classes tend to be transient, their length of stay depending upon their organisational strength, historical ability, and willingness to prevent their absorption into the two main classes. It was Marx's contention that capitalism would simplify class relations, polarising society into the two main classes: *bourgeoisie* and proletariat. This should not be crudely interpreted to mean that every individual would find himself capitalist or worker, but that the great struggles in society would be fought between these two classes. Intermediate classes would be forced to ally with one side or the other, but could never be decisive in the outcome. It has been popular to criticise Marx for the cruder theory, which together with a prophecy of general working-class pauperisation, he put forward in *The Communist Manifesto* (1848). This is not legitimate in view of Marx's later and more mature economic theory of *Capital*.

Against this perspective, it is interesting to examine why Marx could consider that the landlords constituted a class in contrast to his treatment of merchants and financiers. First landlords monopolise the ownership of land, and this intervenes in the operation of the law of value, that commodities exchange according to the labour-time of production. Even if organic compositions of capital are equal across sectors, it no longer remains possible to assume that commodities exchange at their value in the analysis of rent. Secondly landlords constitute within capitalistic production relations the vestiges of the landed aristocracy from feudalism. Finally landlords do not have an unambiguous economic interest in allying with the *bourgeoisie* to raise the rate of exploitation, possibly quite the opposite.

In Britain now we would hesitate before describing the landowners as a class. This is because with the increase of capitalistic wealth, intermarriage, and so on, the ownership of land and capital has become integrated. Also the landowners as a political force have become spent relative to the *bourgeoisie*, a decisive defeat being as long ago as the Repeal of the Corn Laws in 1846. Absolute rent, and even differential rent, could become negative as the *bourgeois* state's taxation eats into it.

Following Lenin's *Imperialism* some Marxists, although not Lenin himself, have argued that finance capitalists (crudely bankers) now constitute a class because of their monopoly of the means of finance. It is clear that such a monopoly could not enjoy the same independence from and antagonism to capital as the monopoly over land described above. Finance capitalists can only form a class for political reasons in order to fight their conflict with industrial capital over the distribution of surplus value. This division of the *bourgeoisie* is not likely to be permanent considering the basic dependence of finance capital on industrial capital and not vice versa, the merging ownership of finance and industry, and their basic mutual interest in raising the rate of exploitation. These remarks reveal a fundamental misconception of much social democratic thought. Labour tends to have a traditional hostility to the evils of 'speculators' and a fear of the power of 'finance-capital' whilst the big industrialists have often remained unscathed by the reformist tongue.

More generally specific distributional relations may generate organised political struggle and temporary classes opposed to industrial capital. Given mobility of capital and labour these tend to be swept aside, possibly leaving pockets of resistance, and their interests have to be represented by or be subservient to organised capital or labour.

10 Marx's Economics and Contemporary Capitalism

Today the world is still dominated by capitalism. This means that Marx's analysis of capital must remain the basis for understanding twentieth-century economic development. This does not deny that capitalism has changed, but the fundamental relations of production are unaltered: the monopoly of means of production and their operating for profit by capital, with wage-slavery for labour.

However, a distinction must be drawn between Marx's general analysis of capital and Marx's *Capital*. The latter contains, besides the former, much that is specific to nineteenth-century capitalism. For example in contrast to Marx's own theory of distribution, most Marxists would agree that in Britain now, it is no longer legitimate to examine land and rent in terms of a landlord class, whilst many would treat finance-capitalists as a class. Nevertheless it should be remembered that Marx's distribution theory holds powerful lessons of method.

A fundamental problem for Marxist economics is to determine the limits of a general analysis of capital. These limits change as capitalism takes strides that it cannot retrace. What is involved is not a few simple propositions of universal truth, nor a massive collection of potential theories, but the drawing out of the ways in which capitalism can operate. Historical experience is of the utmost value. Would Marx argue now that socialist revolution would erupt in the most highly developed economies and that these are the image of the less-developed

71

countries' future? In this final chapter I will construct a general analysis of capital and conclude by suggesting a framework in which contemporary capitalism can be understood.

Central to this is the labour theory of value. This is the expression of the allocation of abstract labour to different branches of production through the social exchange of products that embody concrete or specific labour. It is the social theory of commodity production. Value is the blood running through the veins of the capitalist body, feeding dependent limbs. Many have attacked the labour theory of value for being an inadequate price theory, either because of its limited technical assumptions or because of its basis in the sphere of production (that is to say abstracting from unproductive labour).

One strand of this criticism stresses the impossibility of calculating values, because of constant revolutions in techniques of production, economies of scale, joint production, choice of techniques, 'human-capital', and so on (even apart from data problems). This means that the relationship between value and empirical observation is a complex one, but exactly the same problems exist for any theory that is not a carbon copy of reality. (This is not to suggest that the relationship between theoretical concepts and empirical observation is the same in all theories. Marxism stands on its claim to distinguish appearance – including empirical 'reality' – from reality.)

A stronger basis of criticism of the labour theory of value is the often sympathetic construction of more general theories reproducing the limited 'one-sector' value theory as a special case and with important qualifications. The basic weakness of these theories is that they abstract from the relations of production, so that any advance in the theory, in so far as it has an independent existence, does so also, and is liable to be based in the relations of distribution. But, for Marxists, it is the development of the relations of production that need to be understood and by which distribution relations can be explained. It is value theory, based on the circuit of industrial capital, that embodies the relations of production specific to capitalism.

This seems to suggest that Marxist economics should be

developed by value theory, but presented in a more general framework which is capable of greater flexibility. To some extent this is true as movement is made toward concrete and political study. However, this contains a naïve conception of the relationship between the advance and the absorption of theory. In the limit an obvious danger is the loss of the ability to analyse the relations of production, particularly as capitalism ideologically encourages its radicals to limit attention to the relations of distribution.

Another criticism of the labour theory of value is that it is invalidated by the rise of monopoly. This is an ironic attack on Marx, who would emphasise a tendency in capitalism that destroys his theory of capital. For value theory monopoly poses only distributional complications. In addition the circuit of capital is an excellent framework in which to examine all aspects of monopoly, defined as a barrier to capital in general. This means that some link in the circuit of capital is forbidden to capitalists in general, whether it be due to discrimination, ·monopsony, patenting, or market power. Entry to the circuit at all is always a barrier to the proletariat; a monopoly of finance capital extends this barrier to industrial capitalists.

Monopolisation has also been considered to weaken the social coercive force of competitive accumulation. This view rests on the false opposition of monopoly to competition. It is only by the centralisation of capital into a single hand that competition could ever be eliminated. Thus capitalism must presuppose its reproduction on an extended scale. Also economies of scale cannot be neglected in the accumulation process. This implies that the centralisation and concentration of production form part of a general analysis of capital. Labour will be increasingly socially organised in production in even greater numbers.

The description of crises and the circuit of capital on which it depends must also remain fundamental tools of Marxist economic theory. However, the argument suggested by Marx for examining a falling rate of profit against a rising organic composition of capital and counteracting tendencies is too narrow, appearing to be specific to nineteenth-century capitalism. The general rate of profit calculated according to value is a central category of crisis theory. Its fall must either have profound implications for the rate of accumulation, or offsetting redistribution from those who feed off industrial capital must be forced.

Nevertheless a falling rate of profit depends upon a rising organic composition of capital or a falling rate of exploitation. The attraction of appealing to the former is the almost mechanical causation that it suggests, in particular the apparent independence of the argument from distributional relations, that is, the wage struggle. This is an illusion. The rate of profit cannot fall without an increase in real wage-rates, for otherwise individual capitalists have rejected the profit motive.

However, technical relations of production may be such that the desired rate of accumulation and the rate of profit can be temporarily maintained, despite increased wages, by substituting dead for (more expensive) living labour, consequently increasing the organic composition of capital. Should the rate of profit fall in these circumstances, then no further avenue of escape exists for capital.

Capitalism since the Second World War has enjoyed an unprecedented boom, free from the shattering crises and serious absolute recessions that characterised the earlier *laissez-faire* period and culminated in the depression of the 1930s. Theories that attempt to understand this tend to be mystified by Keynesianism, even if sympathetic to Marxism. Government expenditure is seen as a necessity in the face of the political demands of full employment and demand management. In this perspective the nature of state expenditure can partly be explained by the working-class demand for a welfare state, the indirectly productive services performed for an internationally competitive capital, and the nuclear struggle with communism. This eclectic approach could run on indefinitely, eventually accounting for the last penny grudgingly paid out by social security.

A more satisfactory approach, like Marx's crisis theory, is based on the assumption that commodities exchange at their values, and that there are no disproportions in supply nor deficiencies in demand. Otherwise a crisis is already assumed.

Capital must be analysed by the movement of values not by the breakdown of exchange. All expenditure is liable to increase employment, but in so far as state expenditure employs labour unproductive of surplus value, it is a drain on surplus value. This implies,· *ceteris paribus*, a lower rate of profit and lower potential for accumulation. To make this point clear, if demand management were the purpose of state expenditure, it would be made on capital goods when exercised on behalf of capital.

In Marx's time the rationale for unproductive expenditure out of surplus value was capitalist (luxury) consumption, indirect productive aid to capital, the maintenance of the state, and financial and commercial enterprise. We reject extending this list and adopting Keynesianism as the new rationale of enlarged state economic activity. Our perspective depends upon the self-sacrifice of a group of capitalists in the process of competitive accumulation. It remains to see how that sacrifice is distributed and why it is made.

The answer is to be found in the domination of U.S. capital in the post-war reconstruction. The defence of the western world was not so much against the threat of communist aggression, as the internal revolution that would have been generated by any attempted economic destruction of European by U.S. capital. The United States' withdrawal from competitive accumulation has not been completely altruistic, for where it has lost ground on the roundabouts of accumulation it has gained significantly on the swings – the distribution of produce for consumption. (In this, the United Kingdom has played a subordinate sacrificial role. Recently it has been losing any advantage it had enjoyed in the distributional sphere.)

The exercise of the U.S. hegemony, however, contains the seeds of its own destruction, for it has positively encouraged the success of European (and Japanese) rivalry, and diminished its own competitiveness. Evidence of cracks in the relative stability of the post-war boom – absolute recession, international monetary crises and inflation – reflects the renewal of U.S. participation in competitive struggle. Inflation represents the competition for surplus value between capital

75

and the state. Cost push, demand pull, international transmission and increasing money supply are mechanisms not theories of inflation. International monetary crises reveal distributional struggle. Absolute recession foretells deep crisis.

The preceding argument is subject to much qualification. Groups of capitalists have been seen as represented by nations, despite the upsurge of multinational corporations and the essentially nationless character of capital (as well as labour). The trends discerned are subject to the vagaries of capitalism. However, I want to finish by briefly suggesting the likely outcome of the current phase.

The first consequence will be a distributional struggle of colossal proportions, between classes and between nations. This suggests that any chance of industrial revolution in the Third World will recede into the future. This could have provided a safety valve for accumulation on a massive scale. Secondly a competitive accumulation will be renewed, possibly characterised by a rising organic composition of capital, depending upon labour's success in the distributional struggle. Crises appear inevitable. Finally state expenditure, especially the wasteful, will be cut. Inflation may even be curtailed, unless it is perceived as a weapon for cutting real wages, but not until those dependent on state expenditure have been effectively controlled.

It must be remembered that these conclusions presuppose the economic and political acquiescence of the working class. When their political organisation and consciousness can match their economic strength, the future will herald a new era founded on the revolution and the dictatorship of the proletariat.

MARXIST SOCIOLOGY
Tom Bottomore

In one of the few systematic discussions of Marxism as a sociological theory since Lefebvre's *Sociology of Marx*, Tom Bottomore, the well-known author of *Sociology*, *Classes in Modern Society* and *Critics of Society*, examines the relationships between Marxism and Sociology. But where Lefebvre starts out from the point of view of a justification of Marxism – in which Sociology is treated rather unfavourably – Bottomore considers how far Marxism is itself a useful sociological theory.

Professor Bottomore looks first at the historical relationship between Marxism and Sociology, considering the responses of Marxist scholars to the development of Sociology and the influence of Marxism upon some of the major sociological thinkers. He then goes on to analyse the principal sociological concepts and theories in Marx's work, and the works of the later Marxists; in particular he discusses the notions of class and class conflict; the relations between economy, policy and culture; the concept of ideology; the theory of revolutionary change; and the idea of a socialist society. His conclusion explores the possibilities of new developments in a Marxist sociology.

This much-praised book is bound to be of great value to Sociology students taking courses on Sociological Theory, the History of Sociological Thought, and Marxism, as well as to students of Political Science and Social and Political Philosophy.

The Bottomore is Professor of Sociology at the University of Sussex.

ISBN 0 333 13774 4

MARX AND MODERN SOCIAL THEORY
Alan Swingewood

This book describes and analyses the main concepts of Marx's social theory – alienation, ideology, dialectics, totality, stratification and *praxis* – and relates them both to classical and contemporary sociology as well as to contemporary Marxism. The main theorists discussed are Weber, Durkheim, Mannheim, Schutz, Parsons, Dahrendorf, Lukács, Bukharin, Trotsky and Gramsci. The analysis is not strictly historical or chronological, although Marx's work is set within the specific historical context of his time.

Each chapter discusses a particular concept, its pre-Marxist origins, its role in both Marx's early and later writings. In this way the basic difference between Marx and the other theorists emerges. Marx's social theory is defined as both humanistic and scientific, as both a theory of the objective laws of society and of *praxis*. Interpretations of Marx which define his early work as humanistic and thus ideological, in contrast to his later scientific work, are criticised. Positivistic and scientistic interpretations are also criticised for eliminating the factors of human consciousness and *praxis,* as are other interpretations which turn Marx simply into a humanistic critic of capitalism. Marx's theory is seen as being both dialectical and revolutionary: society is both objective and subjective and is made by men through their *praxis,* and social theory must reflect this.

In general much of contemporary sociology has developed as a criticism, not of Marx's own theory, but of a mechanical and 'vulgar' Marxism propounded by those who came after Marx. By defining Marxism as a form of mechanical materialism Weber, Durkheim, Mannheim and Parsons could thus ignore the genuine theory within Marx's *œuvre*. The crisis of modern sociology has arisen as much out of the failure of modern social theory to explain conflict and contradiction within modern society as it has from the misunderstanding and misinterpretations of Marx's work. This is the basic theme of the book.

Alan Swingewood lectures in Sociology at the London School of Economics and Political Science.

ISBN 0 333 18278 2